the Country Friends® Collection

HARVEST

Mary Elizabeth ...is looking forward to Apple-picking days.

Holly... can't wait for Fall's big cozy sweaters to come out of the closet.

Kate... has been wearing her Halloween costume since August 8.

TRICK OR TREAT

SEPTEMBER

is here,
jump outta bed
put some learnin'
in your head ...

But before you learn
your north from south,
put some breakfast
in your mouth.

— an inspired poem
by Kate

★ Mom's Homemade Pancake Mix ★

10 c. flour	Combine all ingredients.
3 c. whole wheat flour	Store in airtight container.
3 c. corn flake crumbs	Makes 18 cups dry mix.
2 c. old-fashioned rolled oats	Mixing instructions :
¼ c. sugar	combine 1·½ cups dry mix
5 t. baking powder, rounded	with 1 egg and 1·½ cups milk.
1 T. baking soda	Cook on griddle as usual.
2 t. salt	A+

SEPTEMBER

is a good month to see if you can remember ....

THE PLEDGE OF ALLEGIANCE

" I pledge allegiance to the flag of the United States of America and to the Republic for which it stands, one Nation under God, indivisible, with *Liberty* and *Justice* for all."

★ Public school children have been reciting that simple pledge since 1892.

School Days P.B. and J. French Toast ★

bread slices, divided	Spread peanut butter on 6 slices of bread.
¼ c. peanut butter	Spread jelly on remaining 6 slices. Put 1
6 T. jelly or jam	slice of each together to make a sandwich.
3 eggs	Beat eggs lightly in bowl. Beat in milk,
¾ c. milk	salt & vanilla. Melt butter in big skillet
¼ t. salt	over medium heat. Dip sandwiches in egg
¼ t. vanilla	batter, coating both sides well. Place in hot
2 T. butter	skillet — brown on both sides. Serve immediately. Makes 6 sandwiches.

A+

September Lunchbox Treats

JUST FOR FUN!

LIVEN UP A LUNCHBOX WITH *VEGGIE ROCKETS

··· Thin slices of carrots, radishes & cucumbers threaded on a shishkabob skewer are the rocket body; top it off with a baby corncob on the end. Tuck in a container of ROCKET FUEL DIP for a real blast!

Cut sandwiches with cookie cutters for lunch-box treats ⌒ your kids will think you hung the moon and stars.

HAMWICHES
··· perfectly delicious!

1 loaf frozen bread dough, thawed
2·½ c. fully-cooked ham, finely chopped
1 c. Swiss cheese, grated
1 egg yolk
1 T. water

Allow dough to rise according to package. Punch down; divide into 10 piec Roll each into 5" circle. Put ¼ cup of ham & 2 tablespoons cheese on ea circle. Press filling into dough a bit. Beat egg yolk & water together. Brush on edges of dough. Fold circles in half - pinch to seal. Brush t with yolk mixture. Bake 15-20 minutes at 375° on greased cookie s

4

SLIP A LITTLE NOTE OR ENCOURAGING WORDS IN YOUR CHILD'S LUNCHBOX ONCE A WEEK.

WARRIOR QUEEN KATE

BACK TO SCHOOL!

MARY ELIZABETH'S EARLY SCHOOL-YEAR BRIBE TREAT FOR TEACHER

Dearest Teacher: Here is just a small token of our high esteem for you...

A+ APPLE MUFFINS

½ C. SUGAR

¼ C. BUTTER

1 EGG, BEATEN

2¼ C. FLOUR

3½ t. BAKING POWDER

½ t. SALT

½ t. CINNAMON

1 C. MILK

1 C. APPLES, CHOPPED

2 T. SUGAR

Cream sugar & butter together, and add egg. Sift together flour, baking powder, salt & ¼ t. cinnamon. Add alternately with milk. Fold in apples. Fill greased muffin tins ¾ full. Mix 2 T. sugar with remaining cinnamon and sprinkle over muffins. Bake for 20-25 minutes at 400°. Makes about 10 muffins.

Remember the smell of a brand-new lunchbox? ...a clean chalkboard? New leather shoes?

SEPTEMBER'S APPLE-TIME·

GOOD AFTER A LONG DAY OF APPLE·PICKING... JOANN'S

APPLE GRANOLA

6 c. UNPEELED SLICED APPLES
1 t. CINNAMON
1 c. ROLLED OATS
1 c. WHEAT GERM
1 c. WHOLE WHEAT FLOUR
1 c. SUNFLOWER SEEDS
3/4 c. WATER
½ c. HONEY

PUT APPLES IN UNGREASED 9"x13" PAN. SPRINKLE WITH CINNAMON. STIR TOGETHER OATS, WHEAT GERM, WHOLE WHEAT FLOUR & SUNFLOWER SEEDS. ADD WATER & HONEY ⌣ SPOON OVER APPLES. BAKE AT 350° FOR 45 MINUTES. SERVE WARM WITH MILK.

NOW GIMME SOMETHING GOOEY!

APPLE GLOSS

1½ T. butter
1½ c. brown sugar
6 T. water

Apples & Sticks

Melt butter. Add brown sugar & water. Stir 'til smooth. Bring to a gentle boil; cover & simmer 3 to 5 minutes 'til thin but sticky. Remove from heat. Dip apples & put on greased cookie sheet. Chill 2 hours.

TAKE A BITE · HARVEST A BASKET-FULL · RED and BRIGHT

🍎 Make a family trip to an apple orchard ~ a picking expedition is a memory-maker.

🍎 Green and red apples in a bowl are a beautiful sight to behold.

🍎 Mary Elizabeth's kids love this harvest treat: Core an apple, fill it with peanut butter and top it with raisins.

TRY YOUR HAND AT APPLE BOBBING

...BUT DON'T USE YOUR HANDS!

DID YOU KNOW?

Celts would bob for apples as part of their end-of-summer celebration.

★

Folklore has it that if you can get an apple out of the tub without using your hands, you'll have a full year of good luck.

It's FUN

to get together and have Something **GOOD** to eat at least once a day. That's what human **LIFE IS ALL ABOUT...** Enjoying **Things.**

~ JULIA CHILD

How To Dry Apple Slices

1. CUT APPLES INTO HORIZONTAL SLICES NO MORE THAN 1/4" THICK. (FOR FUN, CUT OUT THE CENTER WITH A MINIATURE ★ SHAPED COOKIE CUTTER.)

2. COMBINE 1/4 c. LEMON JUICE & 1 t. SALT. DIP APPLE SLICES IN IT.

3. PLACE ON PARCHMENT-LINED BAKING SHEETS. DRY IN 150° OVEN FOR 4 TO 6 HOURS ~ TURN EVERY HALF-HOUR.

BREW A POT OF HOT AND BUTTERY CRANBERRY CIDER.

4 c. cranberry juice
4 c. apple cider
3" cinnamon stick

2 T. honey
6 T. unsalted butter cut into slices

Combine cranberry juice, cider & cinnamon stick in a saucepan (stainless steel or enamel). Bring to a boil. Reduce heat ~ simmer 10 minutes. Remove from heat ~ stir in remaining ingredients. Keep stirring 'til honey dissolves & butter melts. Ladle into warm mugs.

...sit on the floor and enjoy.

...And Make A Neat Wreath.

YOU'LL NEED:

- DRIED APPLE SLICES
- CARDBOARD, A LITTLE HEAVIER THAN POSTERBOARD
- HOT GLUE GUN
- GLUE STICKS
- HOMESPUN RAG BOW

1. CUT A CIRCLE OR HEART DESIGN FROM CARDBOARD, NOT EXCEEDING 8" IN DIAMETER.

2. COVER WREATH BY GLUING ON THE DRIED APPLE SLICES WITH HOT GLUE. START IN ONE SPOT AND WORK YOUR WAY AROUND. SAVE THE BEST SLICES TO PLACE ON TOP.

3. ADD YOUR BOW ～ YOUR WREATH IS DONE!

Have a Wreath ★ Making Party!

YOU ARE INVITED
B.Y.O. GLUE GUN

Enjoy September!

TRY TO BE HAPPY IN THIS VERY PRESENT MOMENT; AND PUT NOT OFF BEING SO TO A TIME TO COME : AS THOUGH THAT TIME SHOULD BE OF ANOTHER MAKE FROM THIS, WHICH IS ALREADY COME, AND IS OURS.

—THOMAS FULLER—

★7★
WARM and TOASTY

1.

GATHER A COLLECTION OF *oil lamps & lanterns* TOGETHER.

2.

A BIG BOWL OF FRESH *popcorn*...
GINGERBREAD *cookies*
RIGHT OUT OF THE
OVEN ... WARM BREAD...
*aaaaah! ummmm!
ooohh!*

TOUCHES
THAT WILL COZY·UP YOUR
HOME ALL AUTUMN LONG

10

3. A METAL TRAY WITH *candles* OF VARYING HEIGHTS SENDS OUT A WARMING GLOW.

4. SOFAS PILED UP WITH *ooodles* OF FLUFFY *pillows* — can you say "I'M NEVER GETTING UP!"

5. A PITCHER OF *Sunflowers* ON A *Homespun* TABLECLOTH — JUST LIKE PURE SUNSHINE.

6. LOTS OF QUILTS & *Blankets* TO HANG OVER THE ARM OF A CHAIR, A CUPBOARD DOOR... or TO WRAP AROUND *you.*

I FEEL COZY, OH SO COZY...

7. A COZY TRIO OF LITTLE *Log Cabins* ON THE MANTEL SAYS HOME.

I am searching for that which every man seeks — *Peace* and *Rest.*

-DANTE ALIGHIERI-

October

...time to
PicK A pumpkin!

(or six, or
even eight)

Take A
picnic to
the PATCH...

Bring
home a
nice BiG
orange one
for an
elderly
neighbor.

how 'bout a
thermos full of
**WHITE HOT
CHOCOLATE**

3 c. MILK
2/3 c. WHITE
    CHOCOLATE CHIPS
1 t. VANILLA
½ t. ALMOND EXTRACT

Heat milk 'til simmering
Heat 1 c. milk 'til hot ~ not
simmering. Add chips. Stir
in remaining milk & whisk.
Add extracts & remove from
heat.

Have
FUN.

12

The beauty that shimmers in the yellow afternoons of October, who could ever clutch it?
—RALPH WALDO EMERSON

ROASTED PUMPKIN SEEDS

2 c. seeds
1 T. oil
½ t. salt
....

Rinse pumpkin seeds—dry on paper towels. Toss with oil. Place on baking sheet and bake at 350° for 20 minutes. Toss every 5 to 7 minutes. Remove from oven when golden brown. Salt ... eat up!

PUNKIN' HEAD ☺ PIES

Next time you make a pumpkin pie, give it a Jack O'Lantern crust. Simply make the pie as usual, but roll out an extra crust to top it off. Cut a Jack O'Lantern face in the top crust, lay it on the pie, crimp the edge and bake. FUN!

13

WHAT AN IDEA!

★ Carve leaf designs & stars into your pumpkin. You can press the designs in with a cookie cutter or cut 'em out freehand.

★ Sprinkle the inside of your Jack O'Lanterns with pumpkin pie spice ~ smells delicious, especially when the candle is lit.

★ Coat the cut edges of your pumpkin with petroleum jelly to reduce shriveling.

★ "GILD" your gourds & pumpkins with a light coat of gold or copper spray paint.

Kate's PUNKIN' POKES

You Need :
• TIN SHEETS THAT CAN BE CUT WITH SCISSORS
• WIRE
• SCISSORS
• WIRE CUTTERS
• HOT GLUE GUN & HOT GLUE STICKS

1. DRAW STAR DESIGNS ON THE THIN TIN SHEETS.
2. CUT 'EM OUT (careful! They may be rough-edged!)
3. CUT DESIRED LENGTHS OF WIRE... Some short, some long, some straight, some coiled into curlicues....
4. USE GLUE GUN TO ATTACH STAR SHAPES TO WIRES.
5. POKE 'EM IN A PUNKIN'!

14

BLACK CATS and GOBLINS and GHOSTIES...

OH·MY!

BLACK CATS are thought to be envoys for witches, sent to do evil deeds....

Creepy!

KNOCK· KNOCK...

uh, who's there?

Knocking on wood will keep evil spirits away! Folklore also prescribes ringing a bell on Halloween to scare away goblins.

OCTOBER is good for a SCARE!

DO YOU KNOW HOW TO TELL WHEN A GHOST IS NEARBY?

LIGHT A CANDLE & WATCH THE FLAME... IF IT TURNS BLUE, CALL THE SPOOK PATROL!

Gimme CANDY.

COUNTRY ★ FRIENDS® TIPS FOR NOVICE HAYRACK RIDERS:

★ wear appropriate clothing:
- denim jeans so prickly hay can't stab you in the behind!
- a warm turtleneck so bats can't bite your neck
- coat, hat & mittens (BABY, IT'S COLD OUTSIDE)
- Thick socks

★ don't forget:
- a flashlight (to scare away evil spirits or if the tractor gets stuck)
- a thermos of warm cocoa
- emergency candy in case you're stranded!

Harvest Moon Hayride

The October sky is bright with stars...
all aboard for a chilly excursion
under a Jack O' Lantern moon!

THE TREES are in
THEIR AUTUMN BEAUTY,
THE WOODLAND
PATHS ARE
DRY,
UNDER THE
OCTOBER TWILIGHT
THE WATER
MIRRORS A
STILL SKY.
—YEATS—

A MUST·HAVE FOR EVERY

BRING ALONG A STORY-TELLER & A SPOOKY TALE!

NOW WHAT WOULD REALLY BE SCARY IS IF YOU FORGOT TO BRING ALONG

KATE'S BONFIRE CHOCO·CHIP CAKE

⭑ Don't forget your BLANKET & Gloves

1 PKG. CHOCOLATE CAKE MIX, 2-LAYER SIZE
1 SMALL PKG. INSTANT CHOCOLATE PUDDING MIX
3/4 C. OIL
8-OZ. CARTON SOUR CREAM
3 EGGS
1 C. WATER
1 C. CHOCOLATE CHIPS
POWDERED SUGAR

IT SERVES 16 ... (maybe)

IN A BIG BOWL, COMBINE ALL INGREDIENTS BUT CHOCOLATE CHIPS & POWDERED SUGAR. BEAT ON LOW SPEED 30 SECONDS, THEN ON MEDIUM TO HIGH SPEED 2 MINUTES. BATTER WILL BE THICK. STIR IN CHIPS BY HAND. POUR BATTER INTO GREASED & FLOURED 10" FLUTED TUBE PAN. BAKE AT 350° FOR 1 HOUR OR 'TIL PICK INSERTED IN CENTER COMES OUT CLEAN. COOL CAKE IN PAN FOR 15 MINUTES. REMOVE & COOL-SIFT WITH POWDERED SUGAR.

HAYRIDE: LOTS of FRIENDS!

The PERFECT HAYRIDE PICNIC BASKET CONTAINS JUST ENOUGH FOR A DESTINATION

Weenie Roast!

★ LONG STICKS
★ WEENIES & BUNS
★ CONDIMENTS
★ CHIPS
★ WARM DRINKS

Vickie's BEANIE CASSEROLE

...YUMMY ACCOMPANIMENT FOR A WEENIE MEAL!

- 1 T. OIL
- 1 c. ONION, chopped
- ½ t. GARLIC POWDER
- ½ c. CATSUP
- 15½-oz. CAN BUTTER BEANS, drained
- ½ c. BROWN SUGAR

- 15-oz. CAN KIDNEY BEANS, drained
- 2 T. VINEGAR
- 18-oz. JAR BAKED BEANS
- 1 T. DIJON MUSTARD
- ½ LB. CANADIAN-STYLE BACON, DICED

Sauté onion in oil. Combine all ingredients, including cooked onion. Mix thoroughly. Pour into 2-qt. casserole dish. Bake at 350°, uncovered, for 1½ hours, stirring after 1 hour. Serves 9.

Why is it that HOT DOGS always taste better outdoors?

There is no season when such PLEASANT and sunny spots can be lighted on, and produce so pleasant an effect on the feelings, as now in OCTOBER.

-HAWTHORNE-

Enjoy Autumn's pleasures

YOU CAN EAT BY CANDLELIGHT OR FIRESIDE ON THE FIRST CHILLY EVENING.

SLIP A BULKY SWEATER OVER YOUR TEE SHIRT~ aaaah!

WATCH THE SQUIRRELS GET READY FOR A COLD SNAP.

PLANT TULIP BULBS IN THE FALL SUNSHINE FOR NEXT SPRING'S BOUQUETS.

USS KATE

ROW OUT ON THE POND ONE LAST TIME.

Take A Walk on an Autumn Afternoon

POP THIS QUICK OCTOBERFEST DISH IN THE OVEN...WHILE YOU'RE OUT ON YOUR WALK, IT'LL BE SIMMERING!

BAVARIANA CASSEROLE

1 LB. MILD SMOKED SAUSAGE OR BRATWURST
1 LG. ONION, chopped
2 APPLES, PEELED & QUARTERED
27-OZ. CAN SAUERKRAUT, drained
1 c. WATER
½ c. BROWN SUGAR
2 t. CARAWAY SEEDS

...

IN a skillet, cook sausage & onion until onion is tender & meat is browned. Drain.
Stir in remaining items.
Transfer to 2½ qt. baking dish.
Cover & bake at 350° for 45 to 60 minutes.
Serves 6 to 8.

Take along a basket and gather Nature's Treasures for

Autumn Forest Potpourri

...Beautiful in a wooden Bowl!

20 drops orange & spice oil
5 drops bayberry or evergreen oil
7½ c. natural fillers, such as:
- small oak leaves
- pinecones
- acorns
- juniper berries
- chinese lanterns
- dried orange peel
- small seed heads
- oak moss

...

Mix dried materials with oils in big paper bag. Place in wide-mouth canning jar—cover tightly & store in cool, dark spot. check after 2 days — add more oil if need be. Let cure about 6 weeks, shaking occasionally.

21

Country Friends® Ideas for

THE FESTIVE

FALL TABLE

March pumpkins right down the middle of the table.

Use a gold marker to write your guests' names on red apples or colorful gourds ~ clever "placecards."

Tin cans with their vibrantly hued labels are smashing country vases for small mum bouquets. Try one at every plate, or a whole collection of tins for a centerpiece.

PUMPKIN

Fill tall urns & baskets with nature's bounty for primitive beauty at the table:

- twigs & branches
- wheat
- wild grasses
- feathers
- sunflower dried seed heads

KATE'S RUSTIC
NO♥SEW
TABLE RUNNER

EASY! Here's what you need:
- BURLAP, cut to desired size
- 2" TO 5" WIDE RIBBON
- FABRIC GLUE OR HOT GLUE GUN
- IRON
- SCISSORS
- CLIP CLOTHESPINS

OK! FIRST, FIGURE OUT HOW MUCH RIBBON YOU NEED BY MEASURING THE OUTSIDE EDGES ALL AROUND YOUR RUNNER — ADD 6" OR SO.

NEXT, FOLD THE RIBBON IN HALF, WRONG SIDES TOGETHER. PRESS WITH HOT IRON.

NOW SLIP THE FOLDED RIBBON OVER THE BURLAP'S RAW EDGE & GLUE INTO PLACE. START IN THE MIDDLE, I'M TELLING YA IT'S EASIER. USE CLOTHESPINS TO HOLD THE RIBBON IN PLACE WHILE THE GLUE DRIES. YOU'LL HAVE TO FUSS A LITTLE WITH THE CORNERS, BUT IT'S NO BIG DEAL.

— Neat, Huh?

Beautiful Decorations From the Grocery Store?

IT'S TRUE! PUSH YOUR SHOPPING CART DOWN THE PRODUCE AISLE FOR GORGEOUS, NATURAL TABLE DECORATIONS THIS FALL:

Artichokes can be neat candleholders for votives when hollowed out!

Fruit in a big wooden bowl, or arranged on the mantel with pinecones & leaves, looks classic ∼ try apples, pears & grapes.

A crystal compote or cake plate filled with **C**ranberries is beautiful. "Plant" a white pillar candle in their midst.

More to Try:
- NUTS in a shallow clay pot
- REDSKIN POTATOES in a crock
- LIMES & ORANGES piled up on a white platter
- A CORNUCOPIA OF GOURDS & CHILI PEPPERS

23

Here comes November!

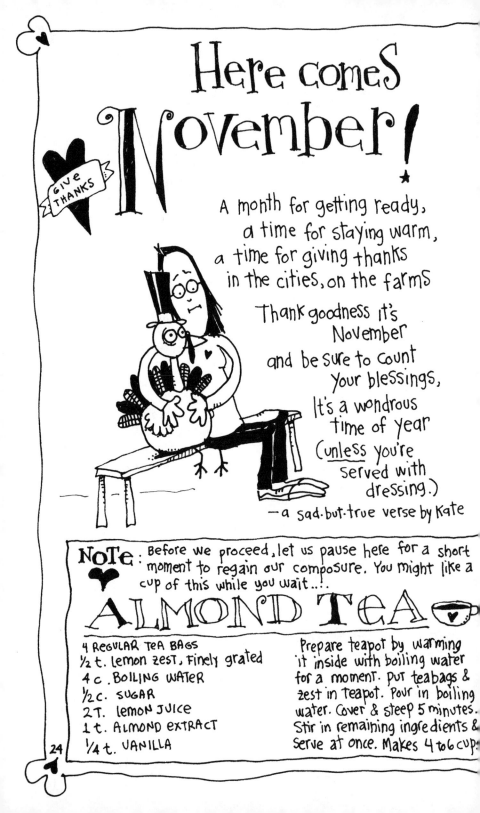

GIVE THANKS

A month for getting ready,
a time for staying warm,
a time for giving thanks
in the cities, on the farms

Thank goodness it's
November
and be sure to count
your blessings,

It's a wondrous
time of year
(unless you're
served with
dressing.)

—a sad-but-true verse by Kate

NOTE: Before we proceed, let us pause here for a short moment to regain our composure. You might like a cup of this while you wait...

ALMOND TEA

4 REGULAR TEA BAGS
½ t. lemon zest, finely grated
4 c. BOILING WATER
½ c. SUGAR
2 T. lemon juice
1 t. ALMOND EXTRACT
¼ t. VANILLA

Prepare teapot by warming it inside with boiling water for a moment. Put teabags & zest in teapot. Pour in boiling water. Cover & steep 5 minutes. Stir in remaining ingredients & serve at once. Makes 4 to 6 cups.

✷ GET READY, ✷ HERE COME THE ✷ HOLIDAYS!

MARY ELIZABETH'S GOOD IDEAS ON GETTING A HOLIDAY HEAD✷ START

Make up your favorite pie pastry ahead of time. Roll it out... put it in the pieplate... cover with wax paper... and hide it in an air-tight freezer bag. Pop it in the freezer 'til you need it. One _less_ thing to do!

Many side dishes can be made ahead of time and frozen. Prepare dishes in the pan they'll be baked in. Cover with plastic wrap, then aluminum foil. On a piece of masking tape, label it with name, oven temperature & baking time. _Aren't you clever?_

Delegate, delegate, delegate! Don't be bashful about asking Aunt Edna to be your yam person, or requesting a veggie dish from Cousin Pearl. Just be sure to ask ahead of time (and remember, don't ask Kate to cook _anything_.)

You've got to be very careful if you don't know where you are going, because you might not get there. —YOGI BERRA

The first sure symptom of a mind in health, is

Rest of Heart, and Pleasure felt at home.

– Edward Young –

Lovely November decorations!

GIVE THANKS

WHEAT Topiaries

FOR THE MANTEL OR THANKSGIVING TABLE

¼" wooden dowels
bundle of wheat
clay pots
raffia
florist's dry foam
assorted dry moss
glue gun & hot glue sticks
paddle wire

STEP 1: CUT FOAM TO FIT INSIDE POT; SECURE IT IN POT.

STEP 2: CUT DOWEL TO DESIRED HEIGHT. USING PADDLE WIRE, START SECURING WHEAT TO THE DOWEL BY ADDING SEVERAL PIECES OF WHEAT & WRAPPING WITH THE WIRE. KEEP ADDING WHEAT 'TIL IT LOOKS RIGHT. LEAVE AT LEAST 1" OF DOWEL UNCOVERED AT THE BOTTOM.

STEP 3: PRESS WHEAT-COVERED DOWEL INTO FOAM. ADD A LITTLE HOT GLUE TO HELP KEEP IT ALL IN PLACE.

STEP 4: HIDE THE FOAM BY HOT-GLUING THE MOSS ON IT.

STEP 5: WRAP RAFFIA AROUND WHEAT STEMS IF YOU WISH!

Harvest Simmering Potpourri

· makes your whole ouse smell fabulous!

6 to 8 dried apple slices
2 whole allspice
1 star anise
2 cinnamon sticks, broken
1 T. orange peel pieces
½ t. whole cloves

. . . . .

Place in a pan with at least 1 cup of water. Simmer over low heat, adding water if needed.

a wonderful gift!
Make up a few batches of HARVEST SIMMERING POTPOURRI ～ divide into plastic bags and tie closed with a note that says,

"Thanks with all my heart for being my friend ～ HAPPY THANKSGIVING!"

Give Thanks for big and small, short and TALL, everyone, over All ... give Thanks from your Heart.

GIVE THANKS

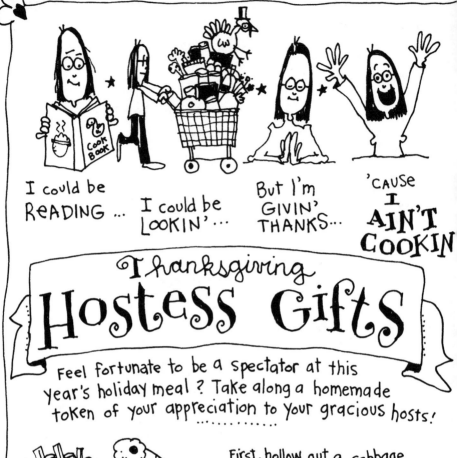

I could be READING ... I could be LOOKIN' ... But I'm GIVIN' THANKS... 'CAUSE **I AIN'T COOKIN**

✿ Thanksgiving
Hostess Gifts

Feel fortunate to be a spectator at this year's holiday meal? Take along a homemade token of your appreciation to your gracious hosts!

DIPPY DAVE
THE VEGGIE BIRD!

First, hollow out a <u>cabbage</u> for Dave's body. Cut a long stalk of <u>celery</u> for his neck, and build a <u>cauliflower</u> head with a <u>carrot</u> beak. (Use toothpicks & wooden skewers to attach all these birdy parts!)

Now, grab a handful of wooden skewers and thread 'em with fresh veggie pieces : <u>cherry tomatoes</u>, sliced radishes & <u>cauliflower</u> florets ... use your imagination. These are Dave's tail-feathers — stick 'em into the cabbage. Attach more <u>carrot sticks</u> & celery sticks with toothpicks amongst the "tail-feathers". Now fill the cabbage "hole" with a delicious dip ⌐ you clever girl!

Sweet 'Tater Bread

THANKS

...You'll love it even if you don't like sweet potatoes! (This recipe makes 5 perfect mini loaves for yummy hostess gifts)

INGREDIENTS:
. . . . .
16-oz. pkg. nut quick bread mix
1 t. CINNAMON
1 t. ALLSPICE
1/4 t. NUTMEG
1/8 t. GINGER OR CLOVES
1 c. WATER
1/2 c. CANNED SWEET POTATOES,
        drained & mashed
1 EGG, beaten
2 T. COOKING OIL
ORANGE ICING
. . . . .

Combine bread mix & spices in big mixing bowl. Add water, potatoes, egg & oil. Stir 'til just moist. Pour batter into greased & floured loaf pan. Bake at 350° for 60 to 65 minutes. Cool in pan for 10 minutes on wire rack. Remove from pan & continue to cool on wire rack until completely cooled. Wrap & store overnight for easier slicing. Drizzle with icing before serving.   ORANGE ICING
. . . .
In a small bowl, combine 1 c. of powdered sugar with enough orange juice (about 1 T. is good) to make it a drizzling consistency.

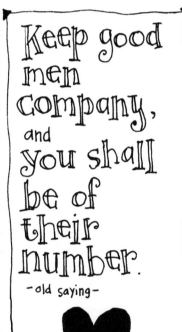

Keep good men company, and you shall be of their number.

-old saying-

Give thanks — for — friends & family.

29

Thanksgiving ♥ Tradition:

Hold hands around the Thanksgiving table.

Make a home video while everyone shares something they're thankful for. (Great fun to watch in years to come!)

Grandma's china & the good silver... and no paper napkins!

Kate ★   Mary E.   Holly

Hold a progressive dinner— put on your coat and move from house to house for each course.

Use a special tablecloth (a sheet works great) and after dinner, let everyone sign it with indelible markers. Use it year after year.

Eat pizza!

Custom, then, is the great guide to human life.
—DAVID HUME

Old & New

Ask your Thanksgiving guests to bring a canned good, or a pair of warm gloves, to dinner... deliver it all to a local shelter for those less fortunate.

Toss a bundle of dried herbs in the fireplace... as you enjoy the fragrance, make a wish for the holiday.

Football on the lawn... Scrabble on the coffee table... parades on the tube.

A special treat for our special friends.

SPOTTY

Kate's annual awful Rutabaga & Fudge Casserole that nobody eats but everybody looks forward to.

If you can't be a good example... then you'll just have to be a horrible warning.

—CATHERINE AIRD—